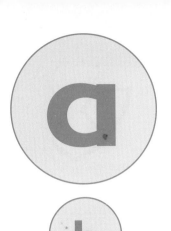

Pictures and letters

Here are some pictures.
Point to each one and say the word.

Here are the first five letters of the alphabet.

a b c d e

Here the letters are jumbled.
Can you circle the first and second letters of the alphabet?

b c e a d

Here is a cat with an apple.

Find another picture

Find another picture the same as the first in each line and colour it in.

Find another letter

Find another letter the same as the first in each line and circle it.

a	c	e	a	b
b	a	e	d	b
c	d	c	d	a

Make the pictures the same

Look at the pictures.
Can you make the animals in each row the same?

Make the letters the same

Look at these letters.
Make the second letter look like the first letter.

d	a
a	c
e	c
d	c

The word 'butterfly' starts with **b**.

Once upon a time...

Do you know the story of 'Goldilocks and the Three Bears'?
Can you tell the story from these pictures?

Here are the three bears.
Do they look happy?

Odd one out

Find the odd one out in each row and circle it.

Find the odd letter out in each line and circle it.

a a d a a

c c c e c

d d d d b

e a e e e

Tell a story

Look at these pictures.

Can you make up a story to go with the four pictures?

What would you call your story?

Let's start at the very beginning...

All letters have different sounds.
These things start with the letter **a**.

apple   ant

Say the letter sound at the beginning of each word.

Busy bee

Say the letter sound at the beginning of each word.

ball   bed   bag

Can you think of other words that begin with
the **b** sound?

Note to parent:
The letter sounds are 'a', 'buh' and 'kuh';
The letter names are 'ay', 'bee' and 'see'.

a b c a b c a b c a

I spy

I spy with my little eye, things beginning with **c**.
Point to the pictures and say the words.

car   cat   comb

At the beginning

Draw a line to join each picture to the first letter of its name.

a   b   c

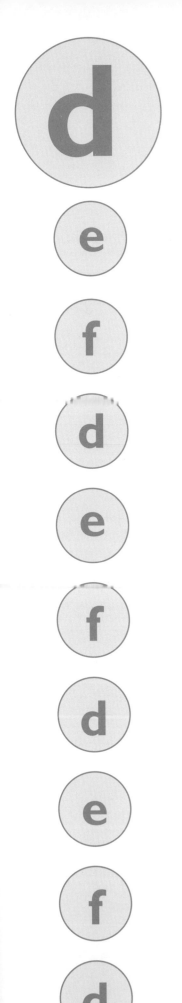

d e f

Look at the pictures.
Say the letter sound at the beginning of each word.

d e f

Draw lines to connect the pictures with the correct first letter.
Can you draw more things that begin with **d**, **e** or **f**?

I spy

I spy with my little eye, something beginning with…

d

The word 'dolphin' starts with **d**.

Colour f

Colour the things in the picture that begin with **f**.

g h i

Look at the pictures.
Say the letter sound at the beginning of each word.

g
h
i
g
h
i
g
h
i
g

g h i

Draw lines to connect the pictures with the correct first letter.

Do you know other words that begin with **g**, **h** or **i**?

I spy

I spy with my little eye, something beginning with...

g

The word 'glove' starts with **g**.

Colour h

Colour the things that begin with **h**.

j

j k l

Look at the pictures.
Say the sound at the beginning of each word.

k

l

j

k

l

j

k

l

j

j k l

Draw lines to connect the pictures with the correct first letter.

Circle **j** in each of these words.

jug   jelly   jam   jump   jiggle

I spy

I spy with my little eye, something beginning with...

k

Draw pictures of other things that begin with **k**.

Little Lisa likes...

Little Lisa only likes things that begin with the letter **l**.
Colour the things that Lisa likes.

Seeing double

Draw lines to connect the letters that are the same.

f g h i j k

i k f g h j

Look at the pictures and say the words. Trace the first letter in each word.

house

helicopter

hat

Circle the letter **h** in these words.

hop

hot

Sort the shopping

Draw lines to put the shopping in the correct trolley.

Draw a picture of something that begins with **b** in the trolley.

m n o

Look at the pictures.
Say the letter sound at the beginning of each word.

Draw lines to connect the pictures with the correct first letter.

m   n   o

Trace the letters.

n   n   n

I spy

I spy with my little eye, something beginning with...

m

The word 'monkey' starts with **m**.

Colour sounds

Colour the picture that starts with the letter at the beginning of each line.

m			
n			
o			

p q r
Look at the pictures.
Say the letter sound at the beginning of each word.

p q r

I spy

I spy with my little eye, something beginning with...

p

The word 'pineapple' starts with **p**.
Can you see two more letter **p**'s?

Colour r

Colour the things that begin with **r**.

s t u

Look at the pictures.
Say the letter sound at the beginning of each word.

s t u

Draw lines to connect the pictures with the correct first letter.

Circle the letter **s** in these words.

sun   sand   star   snake   swing

I spy

I spy with my little eye, something beginning with...

S

Do you know a long, slithery animal whose name begins with **s**? Draw it here.

Colour t

Colour the things that begin with **t**.

v w x

Look at the pictures.
Say the letter sound at the beginning of each word.

V W X

Draw lines to connect the pictures with the correct first letter.

I spy

I spy with my little eye, something beginning with...

w

Circle the letter **w** in these words.

win   was   web

Colour w

Colour the things in this picture that begin with **w**.

y

y z

Look at the pictures.
Say the letter sound at the beginning of each word.

z
y
z
y
z
y
z
y
z

y z

Draw lines to connect the pictures with the correct
first letter.

a is the first letter in the alphabet. What is the last?

I spy

I spy with my little eye, something beginning with...

z

What sound does a bee make?
Can you make that sound?

buzz

y is for yellow

Colour all these things yellow.

You name it

Can you think of a name for each of these animals?
Each name must start with the same letter as the animal.
A good name for the parrot would be Peter Parrot.

a b c d e f g h i j

kangaroo

horse

zebra

monkey

panda

Peter Parrot

I like...

Ben and Carl like things that start with the first letter of their names.
Draw a line to join Ben and Carl to the things they like.

Ben

Carl

Jenny likes things that begin with the letter j.
What is she wearing that begins with j?

Jenny

What's your name? Draw pictures of things that start with the same letter
as your name.

p is for party

Pete is having a party.
Colour the party food that begins with **p**.

Pete's present begins with **p**.
What is it?

It's in your name

Colour the letters that are in your name.

It's in your name

Can you write your name? _____

From a to z

Now you know all the letters from **a** to **z**!
Start at **a**, and join the letters in alphabetical order.
What have you drawn?

Counting 1 to 10

Blast off!

The number 1 stands straight and tall.
Can you stand straight and tall like number 1?

Point to: 1 star
           1 moon
           1 flag
           the number 1

Trace the dotted lines on the rocket to practise writing the number 1.

Where is the number 2?

This octopus loves the number 2.
Can you draw number 2 in the air?

Count the fish.
Write the answer in the shell.

1
2
3
4
5
6
7
8
9
10

Trace the dotted lines to practise writing number 2.

Count and colour

Count and colour 1 thing in each line.

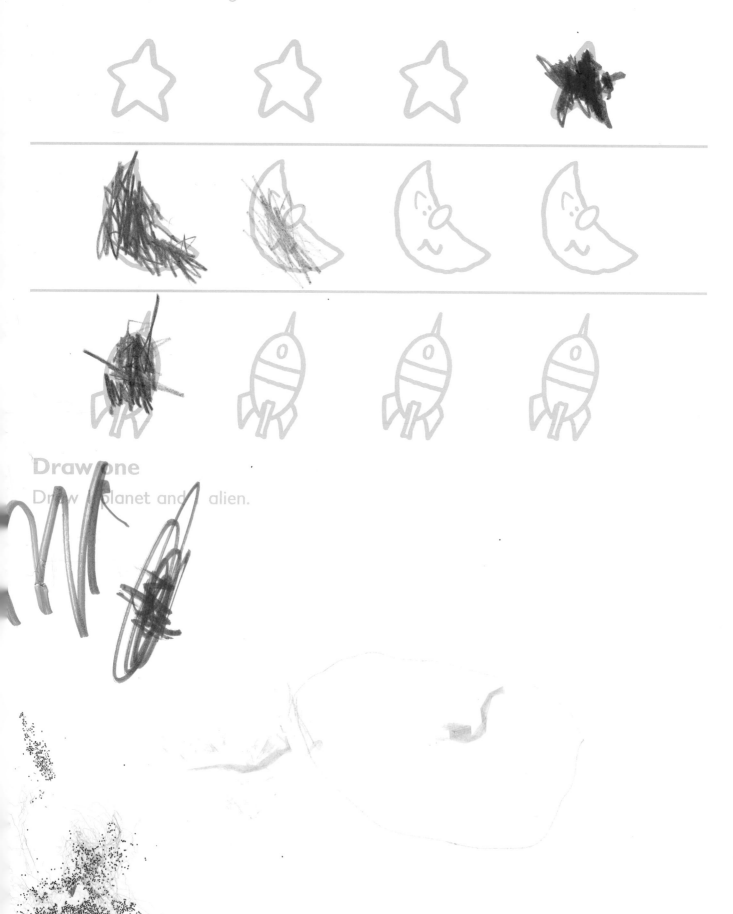

Draw one

Draw a planet and an alien.

Underwater counting

Count the underwater creatures and draw a circle around the number.

1   2   1   2

1   2   1   2

Count and colour

Count and colour 2 things in each line.

It's a 3 snake!

This snake likes the number 3. Wake up
the snake by saying in your loudest voice, "1, 2, 3"!

Trace the dotted lines to
practise writing number 3.

Count the
butterflies.

1 - 2 - 3 are here!

Practise writing numbers 1, 2 and 3 here.

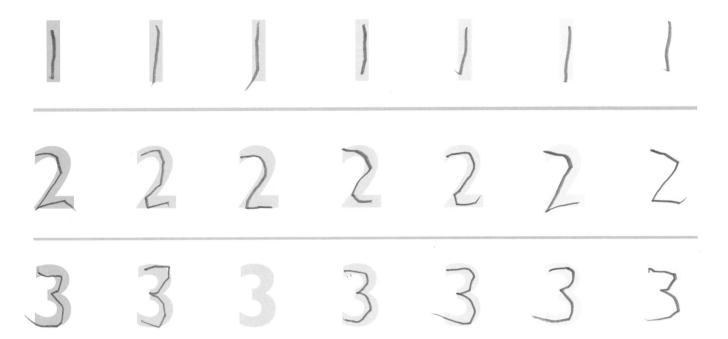

Something is hissing

Draw more things to make 3.

I am a robot!

Switch on the robot by pointing to the number 4!
What shape is the robot's aerial?

Trace the dotted lines
to practise writing
the number 4.

Count the robot's toys.

Robot world

Count the pictures.
Draw lines to join the pictures to the numbers.

1 2 3 4

4s for you

Practise writing number 4.

4 4 4 4 4 4 4

4 4 4 4 4 4 4

4 4 4 4 4 4 4

You're hooked

Do you think the number 5 looks like a hook?
Draw number 5 in the air.

Trace the dotted lines to practise writing number 5.

Count the fish.

1
2
3
4
5
6
7
8
9
10

Dots to spot

Count the dots on the fish. Draw a line between the fish and the number.

1 2 3 4 5

Wobbly jelly

Trace the dots on the jellyfish to practise writing number 5.

Monkey business

The monkey has a tail that curls up at the end like the number 6.
Can you curl up your fingers to look like a 6?

Trace the dotted lines to practise writing number 6.

Making 6

Draw more things to make six of each.

Find the largest

Draw a circle around the largest number in each line.

6	4		5
2	3	5	4
4	2	1	3
1	3	1	2

Spiky 7

Number 7 is a spiky number – just like the spikes on this dinosaur.

Stand up and make your body look like a spiky 7.

Trace the dotted lines to practise writing number 7.

1
2
3
4
5
6
7
8
9
10

Write 5, 6, 7

Practise writing numbers 5, 6 and 7 here.

5 5 5 5 5 5 5

6 6 6 6 6 6 6

7 7 7 7 7 7 7

Count and colour

Count and colour the things in each row.

Dinosaur dig
Look at what the archaeologist has found!

Count the bones.

How many small
bones are there now?

How many large
bones are there now?

Circle it

Count the pictures and draw a circle around the number.

5 6 7

5 6 7

5 6 7

5 6 7

Snow problem

The snowman looks like the number 8!
Can you make a shape like the number 8 using
two fingers on each hand?

1
2
3
4
5
6
7
8
9
10

Trace the dotted lines to practise writing the number 8.

Find the smallest

Draw a circle around the smallest number in each line.

7   8   1   3

2   5   6   7

7   5   3   8

Count and colour

Colour 8 things in each line.

Double ducks

Draw 4 more ducks to go with the 4 already on the pond.

How many ducks are there altogether?

Frogs on a log

Count the frogs on each log and write the number.

Point to the log with the most frogs.

Flutter by, butterfly

Draw a shape like the number 9 in the air.

Trace the dotted lines to practise writing the number 9.

Snail trail

Write the missing number.

Making 9

Draw more things to make 9 in each line.

Creepy crawlies

Draw 4 more bugs.

Draw 4 more spiders.

How many are there altogether?

bugs

spiders

1
2
3
4
5
6
7
8
9
10

Circle it

Count the pictures and draw a circle around the number.

7   8   9

7   8   9

7   8   9

7   8   9

Say cheese

We write the number 10 as a straight line and a circle.

Trace the dotted lines to practise writing the number 10.

Write 8, 9, 10

Practise writing numbers 8, 9 and 10 here.

8   8   8   8   8   8

9   9   9   9   9   9

10   10   10   10   10   10

Count and colour

Count and colour 10 things in each line.

Teds and dolls

Colour the teddies in blue and the dolls in pink.

How many are there altogether?

☐ teddies   ☐ dolls

Toy shop

Count the toys on each shelf and write the number.

Now colour the toys.

Dotty dominoes

Count the dots on each domino and write the number.

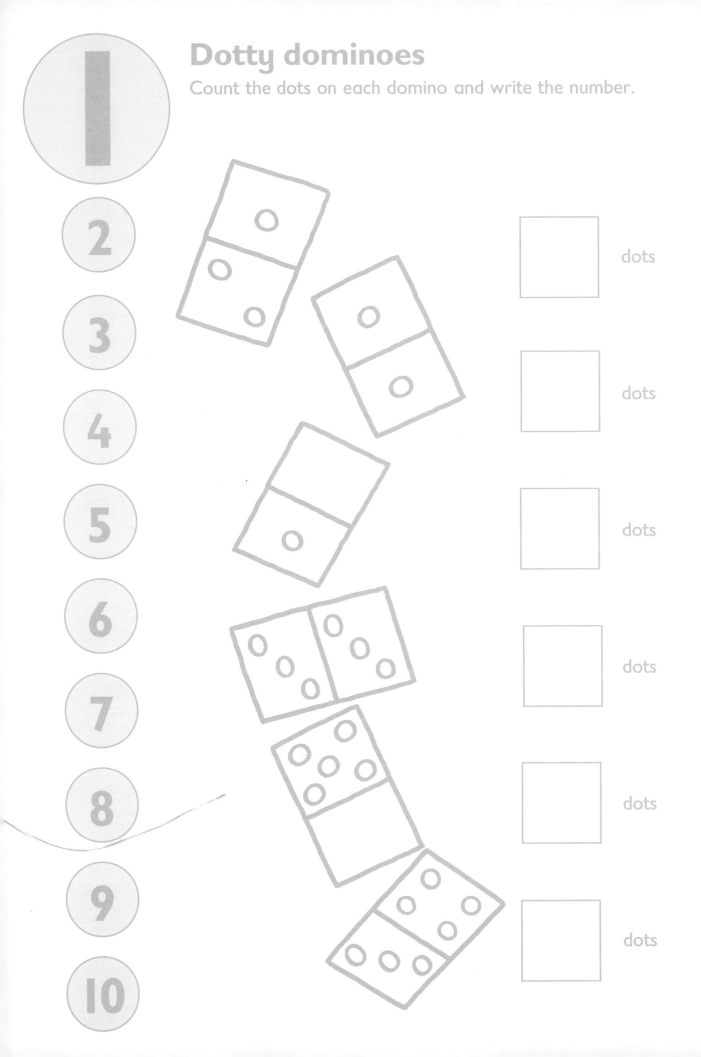

☐ dots

☐ dots

☐ dots

☐ dots

☐ dots

☐ dots

1

2

3

4

5

6

7

8

9

10

Spotty dogs

Count the spots on the dogs.

Draw a line from each dog to the correct number.

Starry night!

Join the planets in order from 1 to 10. What shape can you see?

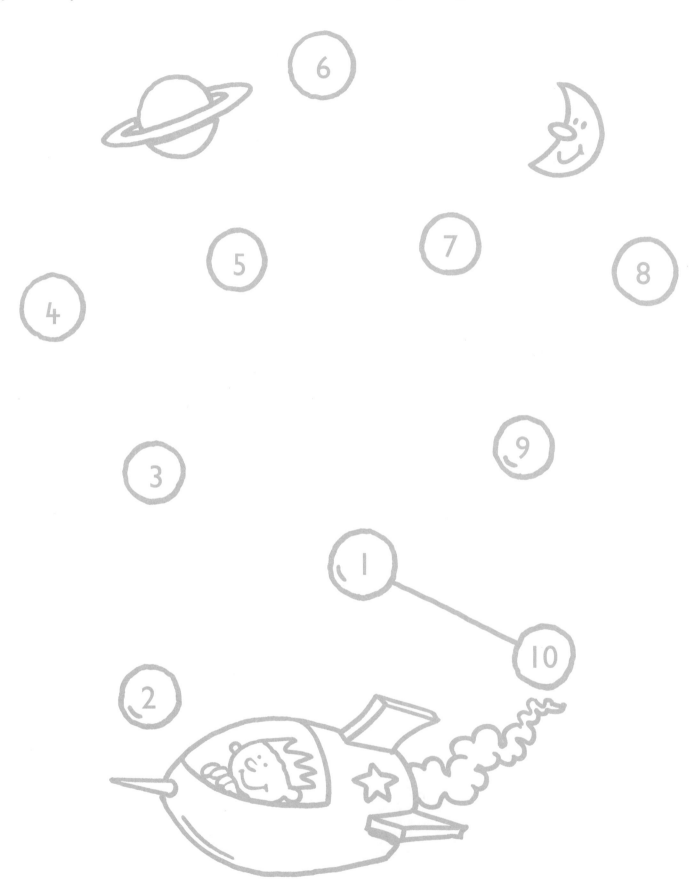

Writing

Straight lines

Lines are everywhere.
How many lines can you see around you?

Trace the lines to draw stripes on the snake.

Trace the lines to draw stripes on the tiger.
Now let's make it rain! Draw rain coming from the clouds
in straight lines.

Down and across

Trace the lines on the roller coaster.

Zigzags

Zigzag lines go up and down, up and down.
Draw a zigzag line in the air.

Trace the lines to draw sharp teeth on the big dinosaur.
Now draw spikes on the little dinosaur's back.

Here comes thunder!

Wavy lines

Trace the lines to draw big waves in the sea.
Draw wavy lines in the sand.

Circles

Trace the lines to draw lots of circles.
Which are easier to trace – big circles or small ones?

Here are some more circles for you to trace.

Do you know which letters use a circle shape?

Straight letters

Can you stand straight and tall like the letter **l**?
All these letters have straight backs.

l i t f k

Can you write each letter in the air? Use your finger like a pencil. Start from the top each time.

Now you are ready for some real writing!
Trace the lines to write the letters.

l is like a stick of rock

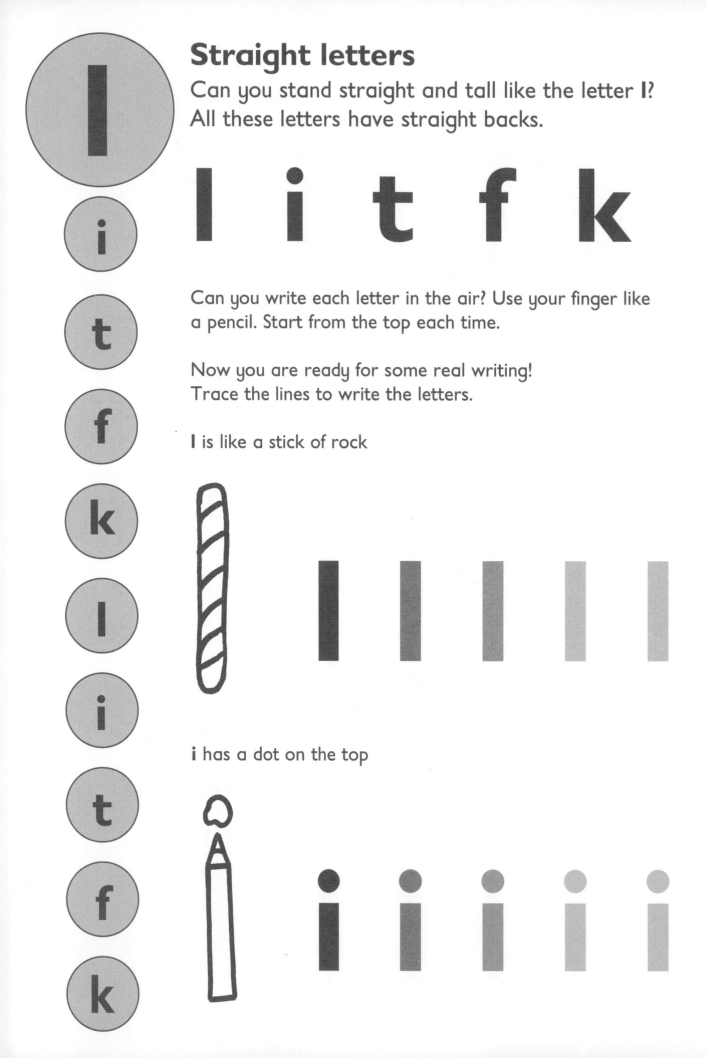

i has a dot on the top

t curls up like an anchor

f is like a flower

k can kick like a footballer

Can you dance like a ballet dancer
or march like a soldier, keeping your
back very straight?

Round letters

These letters have a round shape.

o   c   a   s

Let's write a big round circle in the air.
Start at the top, go down, all the way around and back to
the top! Well done, that was the letter o.

Now try the other letters. Start from the top each time.
Trace the lines to write the letters inside the bubbles.

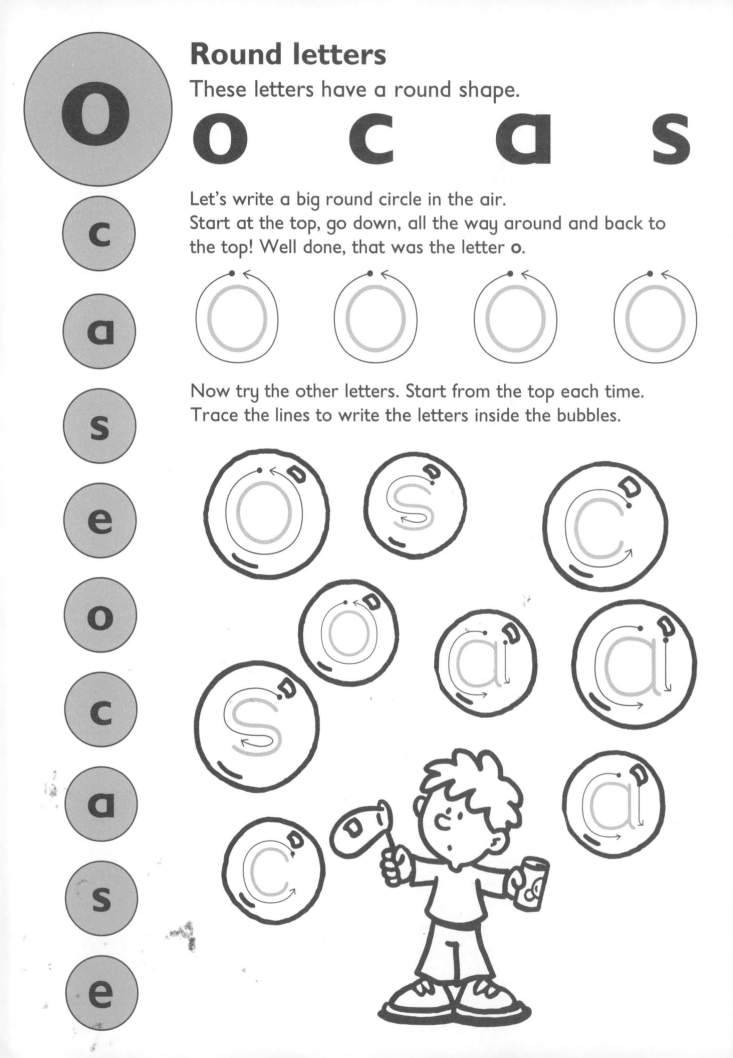

e for egg

The letter **e** is round too, but we write it from the middle — from its tummy!
Can you write an **e** in the air?

Now trace the lines to write **e** inside the eggs.

Do you have any round letters in your name?

b and d

The letters **b** and **d** like **c**.
They always face **c** in the alphabet!

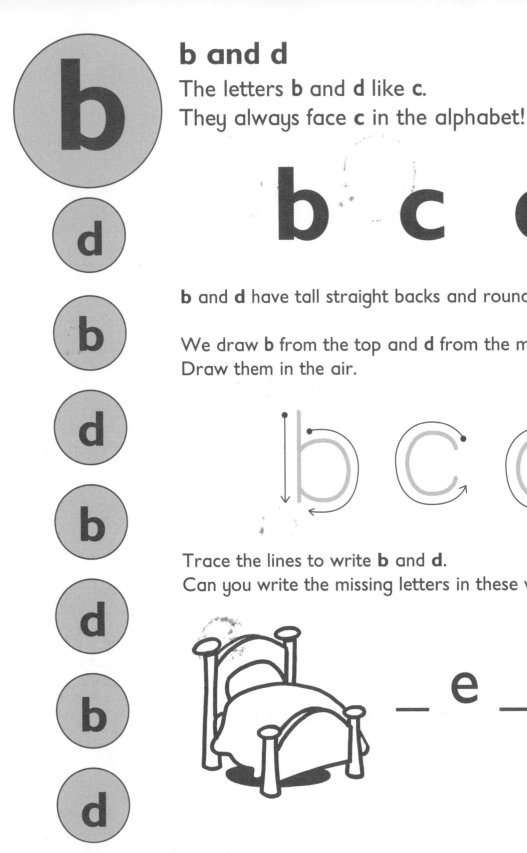

b   c   d

b and **d** have tall straight backs and round tummies!

We draw **b** from the top and **d** from the middle.
Draw them in the air.

Trace the lines to write **b** and **d**.
Can you write the missing letters in these words?

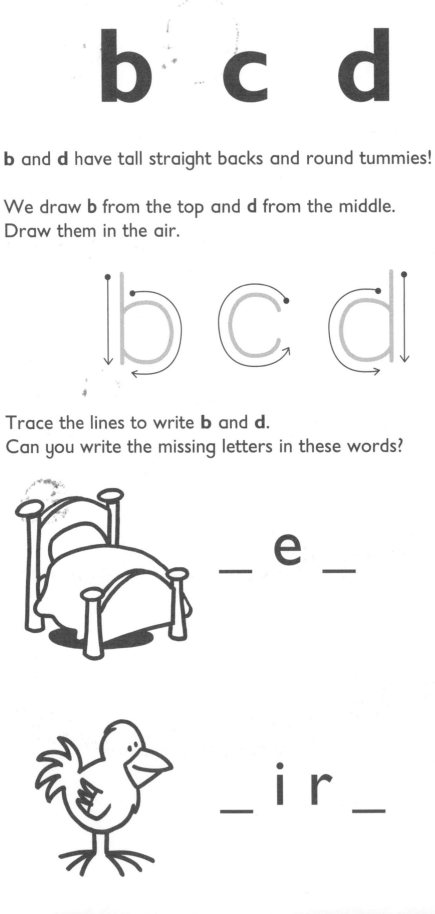

_ e _

_ i r _

Best buddies

b and **d** are best buddies, but each likes different things.
b likes things that begin with **b**.
d likes things that begin with **d**.

Draw lines to the things they like.

Letters with tails

These letters have curly tails.

j g y

Practise drawing them.
Start from the top of the letter. They all curl the same way.

j is like a sock

j j j j

g is like a monkey

g g g

y is like a yacht

y y y

j g y

Trace the letters on the washing line.

j g y j y j g y

Can you write the letters on the washing line?
Their heads go above the line.

p and q

The letters **p** and **q** face each other in the alphabet. One of them has a pointy tail. Which one is it? Draw both letters in the air.

p   q

Now trace the lines to write the letters in the sea. Make sure they keep their heads above the water!

Pat-a-cake

Write the missing p's in this rhyme.

Pat a cake, ___at a cake, baker's man.

Bake me a cake, as fast as you can.

Pat it and ___rick it and mark it with ___,

and ___ut it in the oven for baby and me!

Write **q** on one of the cakes. That cake is for the queen.
Now write the first letter of your name on another cake.
That one is for you!

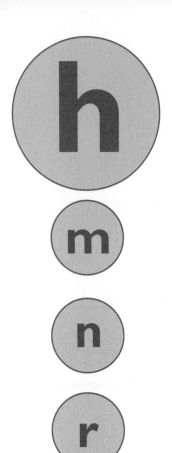

Straight lines and curves
These letters have straight lines and curves.

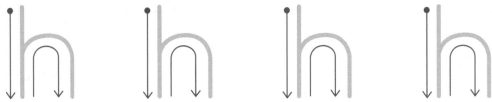

h m n r

They are all the same height, except one.
Which letter is taller than the others?

Can you write these letters in the air? Now trace them.

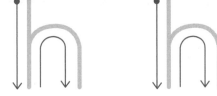

Do **m** and **n** remind you of little round hills?

When you write **m** you go...
down the hill and up the hill, down the hill and up the hill,
and down the hill again!

Jack and Jill are climbing up the
letter **m**.

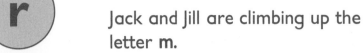

Upside down u

Does the letter **u** look upside down to you?

What letter does **u** make if you turn it upside down?

Write **u** in the air with your finger. Then trace the lines to write the letters.

Can you write the missing **u**
in this sentence?

Una has an
_mbrella!

Different directions

These letters have straight lines that go in different directions.

v is like a candlestick

w is like this table

x is like the thread on a button

z is like a slithering snake

Trace the letters to finish the words.

vest

bow

box

zip

Can you write the missing letters in this sentence?

A bo_ with a bo_.

Copy cats

Trace the letters. Then find a matching letter and draw a line to connect them.

a
b
c
d
e
f
g
h
i
j

s   n   t

n   x

f   e

f

e

s   t   x

Trace over the dots to make a picture of a cat.
Have you drawn a copycat?

Amazing alphabet

Starting at the letter **a**, trace the letters of the alphabet in order, and find your way through the maze.

start

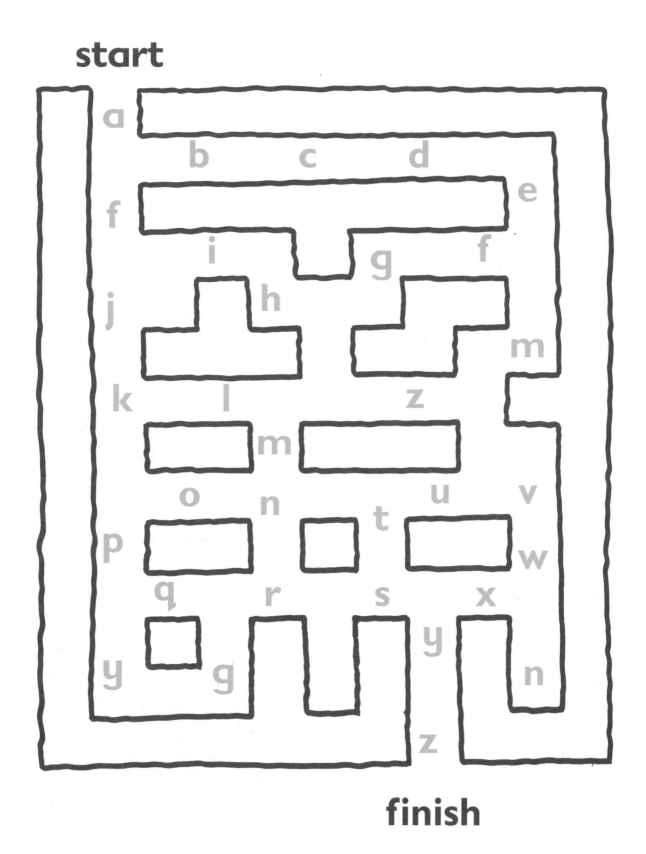

finish

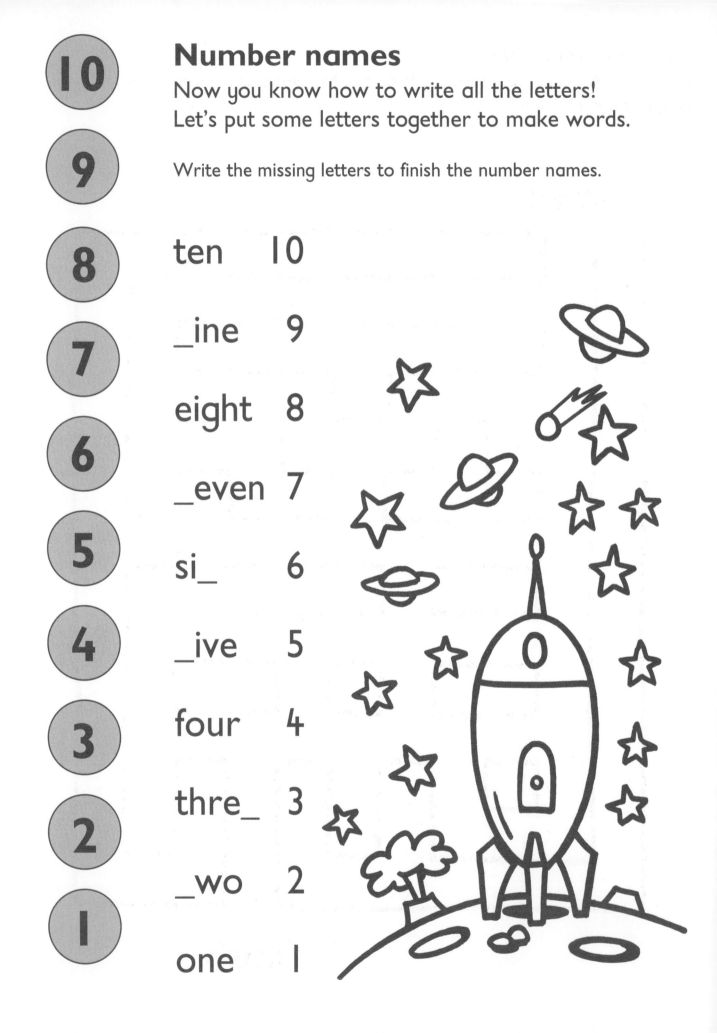

10
9
8
7
6
5
4
3
2
1

Number names

Now you know how to write all the letters!
Let's put some letters together to make words.

Write the missing letters to finish the number names.

ten   10

_ine   9

eight   8

_even   7

si_   6

_ive   5

four   4

thre_   3

_wo   2

one   1

Colour names

Here are some more names.

Write the missing letters to finish the colour names.
Colour in this picture using as many of the colours as you can.

_ellow

_range

_ed

_urple

_lue

_reen

a
b
c
d
e
f
g
h
i
j

This is me!

One very important name belongs to you!
What's your name?

Draw a picture of yourself in the picture frame.
Write your name underneath it in your best writing.

About me

Write words in the spaces.

I am _____ years old.

My favourite word is _____ .

My best friend is _____ .

Which of these things do you like to do?
Write **y** for yes, or **n** for no, in the boxes.

Twinkle, twinkle, beautiful star

Trace the lines to draw a big star.
Colour the star using the letter code.

y = yellow   b = blue
r = red   o = orange
g = green   p = purple

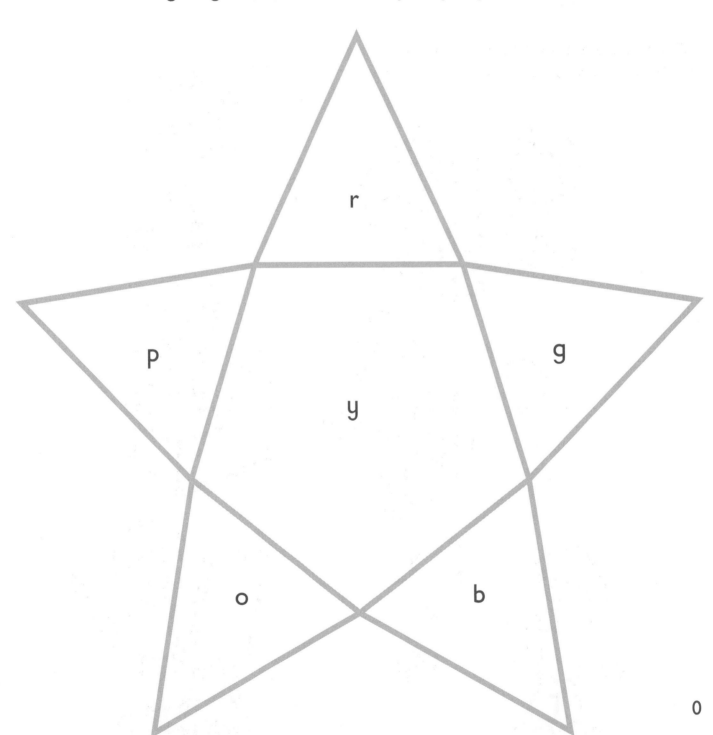

0

Early Maths

1

2

3

4

5

6

7

8

9

10

Get ready to count...
When we have lots of things, we like to count them!
But sometimes it's not so easy...

Octopus tried to count his legs, but he found it was
a knotty problem.

Leopard tried to count his spots, but it made him
see spots in front of his eyes!

Can you help Octopus count his legs and help Leopard
count his spots? Point to the numbers and say them.

Buckle my shoe

There are rhymes to help Octopus and Leopard learn to count.
Here's one of them.

1, 2, buckle my shoe.

3, 4, knock at the door.

5, 6, pick up sticks.

7, 8, lay them straight.

9, 10, a speckled hen.

How many eggs has the speckled hen laid?

What can you see?

Count up to 3, what can you see?

Count up to 3 – birds in the tree.

Count up to 5 – bees in the hive.

Count up to 7 – stars in heaven.

Count up to 9 – clothes on the line.

Count 10 or more – shells on the shore.

How many shells on the shore?
Were there more than 10?

Crazy creatures

How many crazy creatures are there?
Count each line of animals and circle the number.

1 2 3 4 5 6 7 8 9 10

1 2 3 4 5 6 7 8 9 10

1 2 3 4 5 6 7 8 9 10

1 2 3 4 5 6 7 8 9 10

How many legs?

How many legs do you have? Only two!
Which of these animals has the most legs?
Count the legs. Write the number.

bird ☐

spider ☐

fly ☐

beetle ☐

Colour in the animal with the most legs.

Draw more

Draw more legs to make the same number on each insect.

How many legs does a worm have?
None!

Counting down

Write the missing numbers for the countdown from 10 to 1.

Look again!

Here are 10 dots. Can you count them?

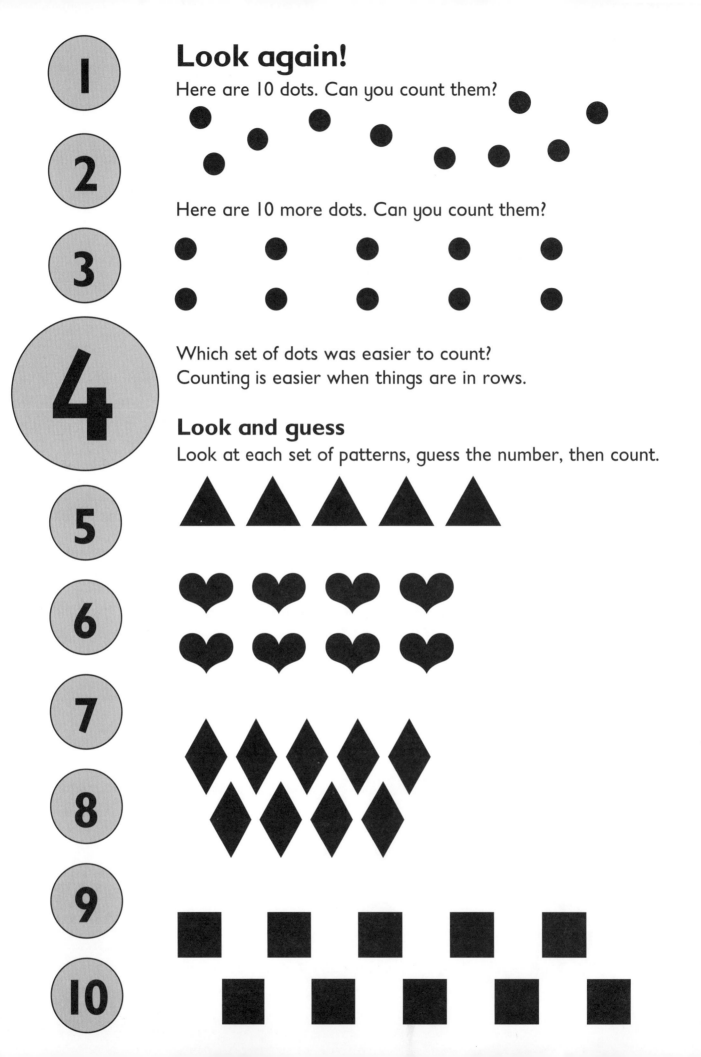

Here are 10 more dots. Can you count them?

Which set of dots was easier to count?
Counting is easier when things are in rows.

Look and guess

Look at each set of patterns, guess the number, then count.

Number patterns

Copy each pattern. Then guess the number and count.
Write the numbers in the boxes.

Find some playing cards.
You will find lots of
number patterns on
playing cards,
dominoes and dice.

Doodle drawings

Draw a picture of your house. Colour it in 3 colours.

Now draw another picture of your house. This time colour it in 5 colours.

Birds of a feather flock together

Birds that look the same want to be together.
Look at these birds. Answer the counting questions.

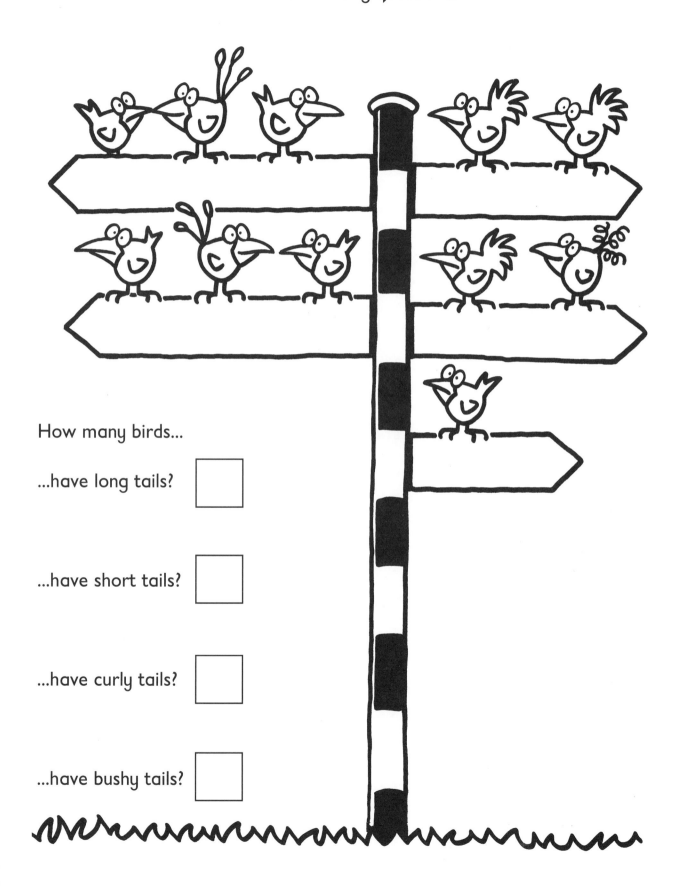

How many birds...

...have long tails?

...have short tails?

...have curly tails?

...have bushy tails?

Looking at shapes

Can you make a circle shape with your hands and fingers? Can you make a triangle shape?

Here are some names for different shapes.

square   circle   triangle   rectangle

Shapes all around

What shape is a plate?
Draw a line to connect the plate to the matching shape.

Draw a line to connect the window to the matching shape.

Robot shapes

Can you see the shapes that make up the robot?

Count the shapes in the robot picture. Write the numbers on the lines.

1

2

3

4

5

6

7

8

9

10

Sorting shapes

Round shapes here. Square shapes there.
There are shapes everywhere!

Colour the shapes with 4 sides yellow.
Colour the shapes with 3 sides blue.
Colour the other shapes red.

How many are there?

yellow shapes ☐

blue shapes ☐

red shapes ☐

Terrible twins

Draw the missing shapes to make the robots the same.

Matching shapes

Colour the two shapes in each line that are exactly the same.

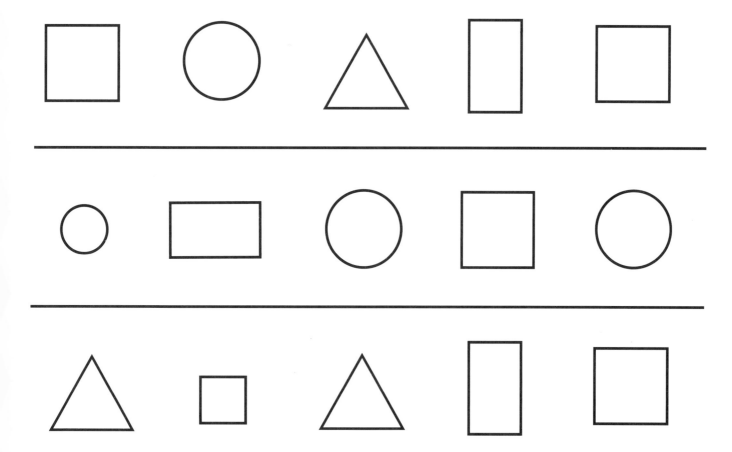

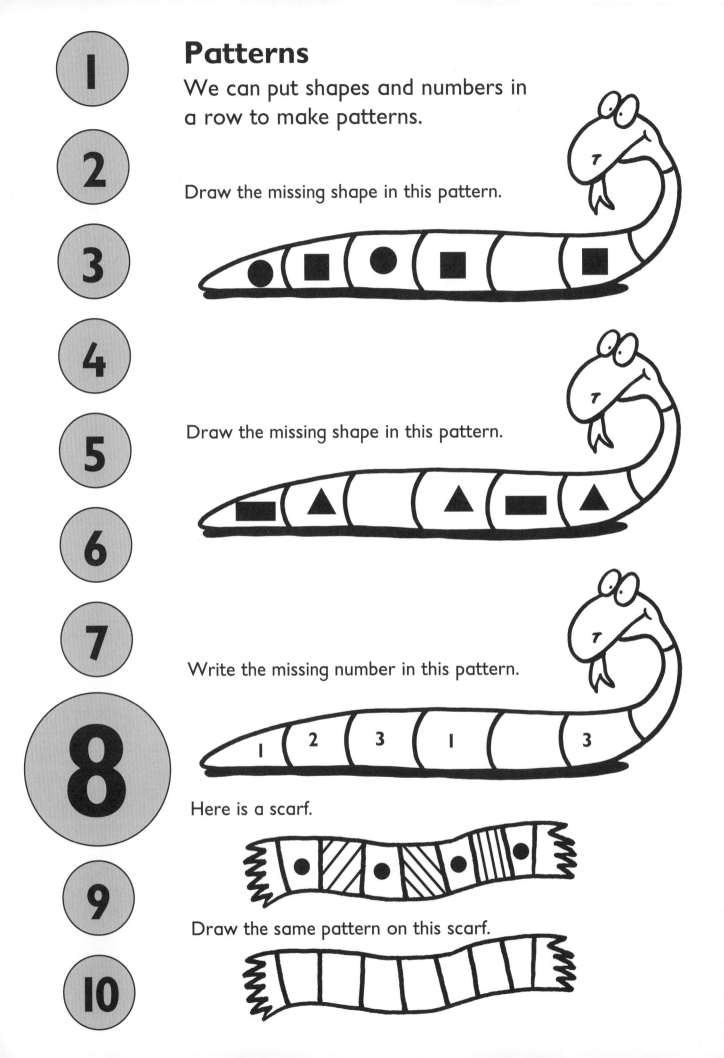

Patterns

We can put shapes and numbers in a row to make patterns.

Draw the missing shape in this pattern.

Draw the missing shape in this pattern.

Write the missing number in this pattern.

Here is a scarf.

Draw the same pattern on this scarf.

Making 5

How many are there altogether? Write the answers in the boxes.

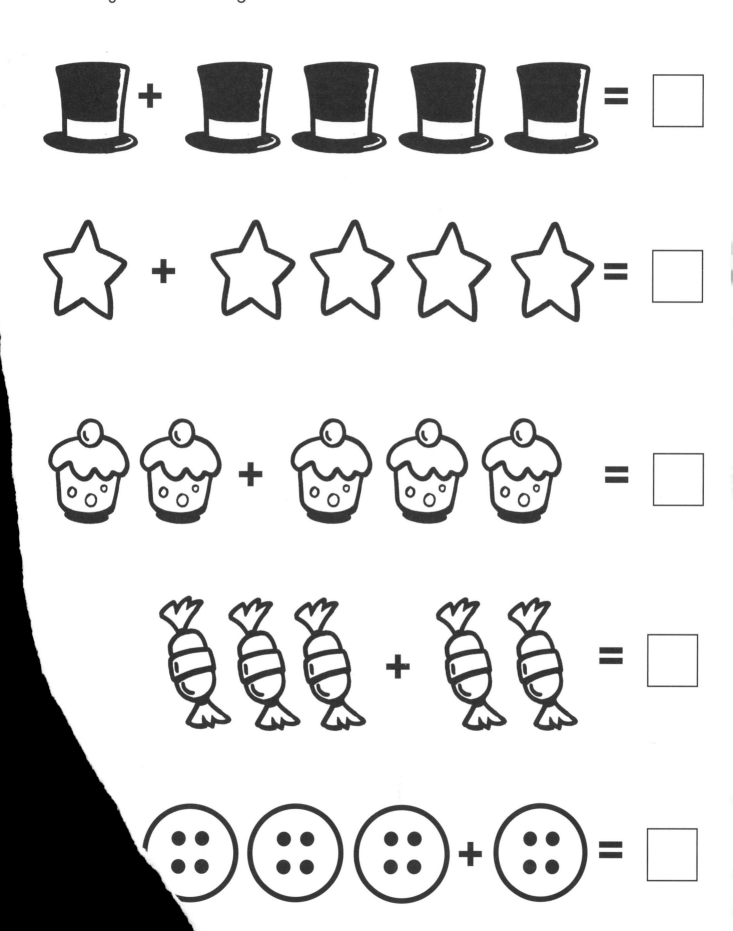

Take away 1

Sometimes we want to make numbers less by taking away.

Take away 1 thing from each line by crossing it out.
How many things are left in each line?
Write the number in the box.

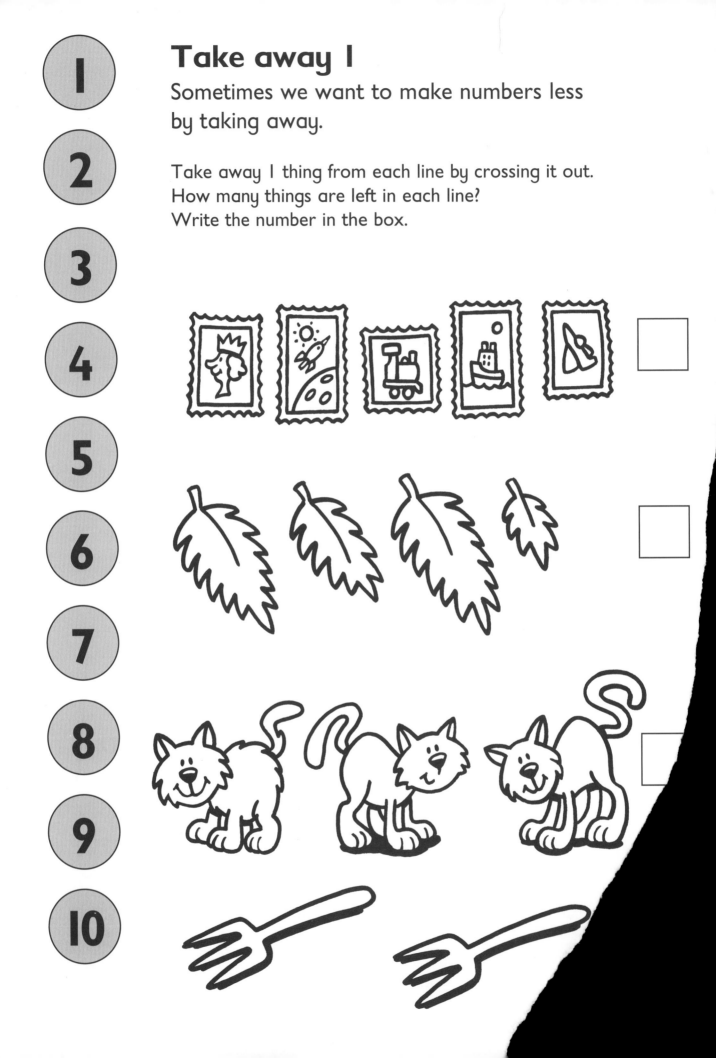

Five teds in a bed

This is a funny song. Can you learn it?

There were 5 in the bed and the little one said,
"Roll over, roll over."
So they all rolled over and one fell out.

There were 4 in the bed and the little one said,
"Roll over, roll over."
So they all rolled over and one fell out.

There were 3 in the bed and the little one said,
"Roll over, roll over."
So they all rolled over and one fell out.

There were 2 in the bed and the little one said,
"Roll over, roll over."
So they all rolled over and one fell out.

There was 1 in the bed and the little one said,
"Goodnight!"

Take away 2

Take away 2 things from each line by crossing them out.
How many are left?

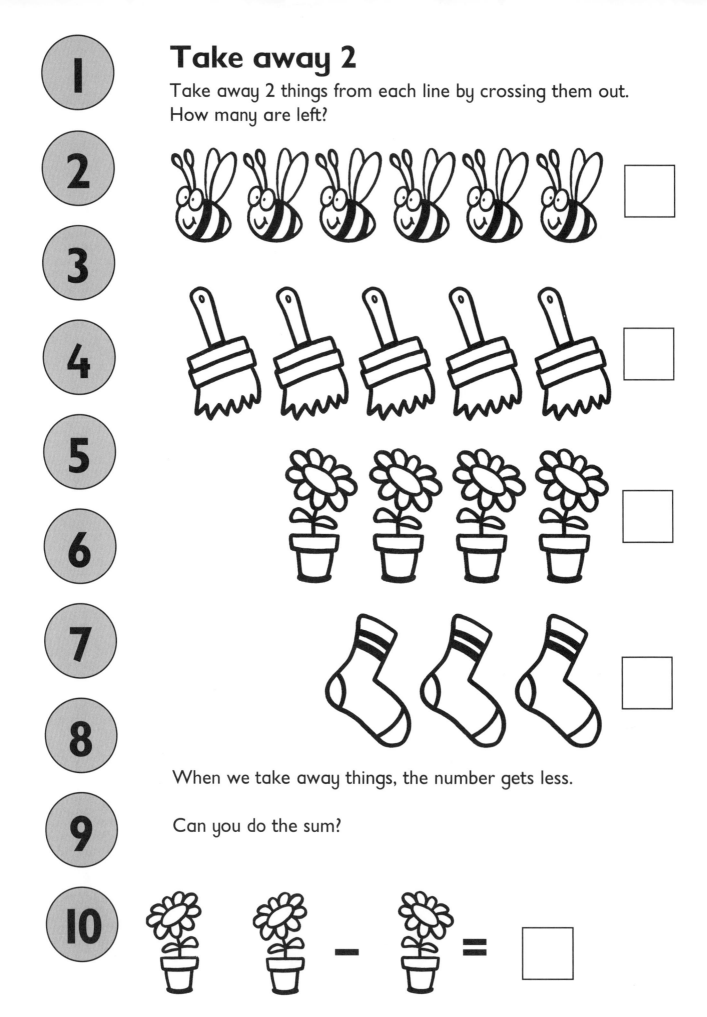

When we take away things, the number gets less.

Can you do the sum?

1
2
3
4
5
6
7
8
9
10

Take away 3

Here are some more take away sums. Take away 3 from each line.
How many are left? Write the answer in the box.

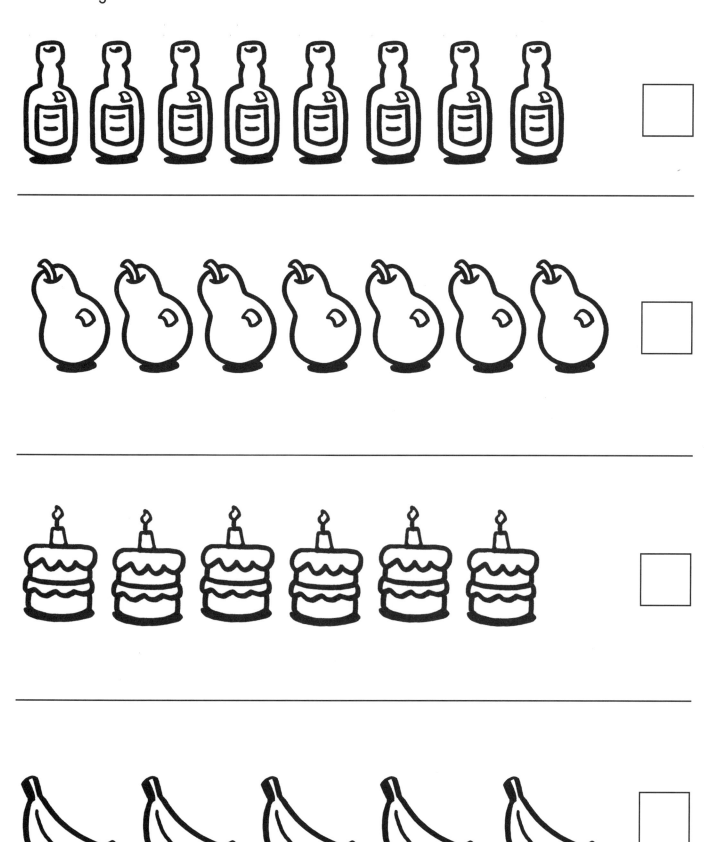

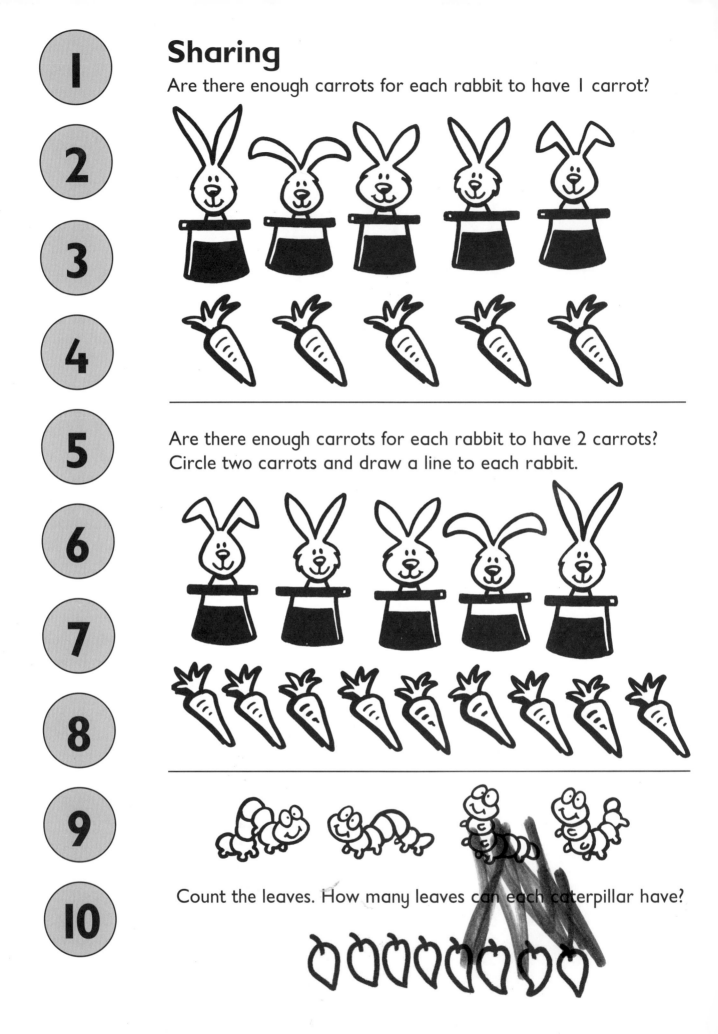

Sharing

Are there enough carrots for each rabbit to have 1 carrot?

Are there enough carrots for each rabbit to have 2 carrots?
Circle two carrots and draw a line to each rabbit.

Count the leaves. How many leaves can each caterpillar have?

1 2 3 4 5 6 7 8 9 10